Trugs, Dibbers, Trowels and Twine

TRUGS, DIBBERS, TROWELS AND TWINE

This revised and updated edition copyright © Summersdale Publishers Ltd, 2018

First published in 2010

Text by Anna Martin

Cover images: leaves, pumpkins, berries, mushroom, grapes, swirls © Skorik Ekaterina/Shutterstock.com; trowel, fork © mart/Shutterstock.com; watering can, secateurs © Macrovector/Shutterstock.com

An Hachette UK Company
www.hachette.co.uk

Summersdale Publishers Ltd
Part of Octopus Publishing Group Limited
Carmelite House
50 Victoria Embankment
LONDON
EC4Y 0DZ
UK

www.summersdale.com

Printed and bound in Poland

ISBN: 978-1-78685-257-1

Substantial discounts on bulk quantities of Summersdale books are available to corporations, professional associations and other organisations. For details contact general enquiries: telephone: +44 (0) 1243 771107 or email: enquiries@summersdale.com.

Trugs, Dibbers, Trowels and Twine

and

Twine

Isobel
Carlson

summersdale

contents

Introduction

'The love of gardening is a seed
once sown that never dies.'

GERTRUDE JEKYLL

Watching a garden grow and flourish under your care is hard to beat. A 'garden' can mean anything from a few much-loved potted herbs on a tiny balcony on an urban high-rise building, to vast acres of avenues, orchards, ponds and vegetable plots in an idyllic country setting. Whilst we would all love to have a garden worthy of inclusion in *The Yellow Book*, the reality is that many of us don't have time to regularly maintain our outside space and would rather, given the choice, use the garden for relaxation than as a place for hard work. The pages of this book should help you get the most out of your garden, whether you are green-fingered or not, and show that even minimum effort and a few quick fixes can reap big rewards. As well as a host of tried and trusted tips, you will find some simple recipes to make full use of your home-grown produce, along with quotations and poems to inspire and quirky snippets of garden lore to intrigue. Learn invaluable tricks such as how to keep pests at bay, grow the perfect carrot, pep up wilting tulips, and even make our more 'friendly' insects feel welcome.

The main message here is to enjoy your garden, however big or small: to be creative; to encourage your friends and family outdoors for picnics, snowball fights and scavenger hunts; to feed the chickens, collect and pot the honey, and appreciate what each season has to offer.

Planning Your Garden

*'If you would be happy all
your life, plant a garden.'*

CHINESE PROVERB

Always adhere to the rule that less is more when planning your garden. The space around the plants is just as important as the plants themselves. A simple combination of lawn, flowerbeds, patios and paths is all you need.

*'"One likes a mosaic pavement to look
like a garden," said Euphrosyne, "but
not a garden like a mosaic pavement."'*

BENJAMIN DISRAELI, *LOTHAIR*

Try introducing curves to your design; it adds a sense of motion and flow to the space and gradually reveals different aspects of the garden. A curved border or low-level hedge, for example, adds a point of interest and an impression of space.

Hide your compost heap and wheelie bins from view by erecting a few trellis panels and growing some attractive climbers that will provide bursts of colour throughout the year, such as clematis in spring, honeysuckle and climbing roses in summer, Virginia creeper in autumn and winter jasmine in winter.

GARDEN LORE...

One superstition states that it is important to keep boundary fences in good order or disputes will occur between you and your neighbours – seems like sensible advice!

Take into account a plant's size on reaching maturity and allow it plenty of room to grow so that it doesn't dominate other plants. Have smaller, flowering plants in front and larger grasses and bushes behind.

To make a small garden appear bigger, plant bright, attention-grabbing colours at the front of the border and cooler ones at the back.

If you have a narrow garden, you can divide it up with hedging or trellising and have separate enclosed spaces such as a formal area, a lawn, a vegetable patch and a place for your compost heap and shed. The separate 'rooms' can be linked by a long, curved path.

'Should it not be remembered that in setting a garden we are painting a picture?'

BEATRIX JONES FARRAND

When looking around other gardens for inspiration, take note of the textures of plants; are the leaves or flowers feathery or spiky? Is the leaf surface glossy, bumpy, fuzzy or wrinkly? Pick a few favourite textures that will add contrast to your garden.

Remember that nature has a way of filling in the gaps in a garden, so unless you are good at keeping on top of the weeding it is best to fill the gaps yourself with attractive bedding plants.

If your garden is very small, give the impression of space by laying a walkway or path that gets narrower as it recedes into the distance.

There is always room to go upward; try vertical planting by adding a trellis to a wall or fence and train climbing roses, clematis or honeysuckle to grow on it.

Adding a bench or a table and chairs into the garden gives an instant feeling of calm. If possible, position the seating so that you can view the sunset, as this tends to be the time when people potter and relax outside. To make it even more special, plant flowers that release their scent in the early evening near to the seating, such as honeysuckle, jasmine and dame's hyacinth.

Installing a water feature, such as a small fountain or pond, can draw attention away from the smallness of the garden surrounding it. It is also an addition that can prove peaceful and relaxing.

Create your own secret garden by building a stone wall, fence or hedging around it. A thick hedge will attract wildlife, offering food and shelter; a well-built stone wall is a natural, enhancing feature which can last a lifetime; and a fence can be easily covered with numerous climbers offering attractive, colourful blooms.

Make a raised bed for your vegetables – it not only eliminates the need for paths and walkways, but makes it considerably less strenuous when tending your crops. If your garden is mainly shady, stick to a floral colour scheme of purples, blues and greens. Conversely, hot pinks, reds and yellows work best in a sun-trap garden.

The kiss of the sun for pardon,
The song of the birds for mirth,
One is nearer to God's heart in a garden
Than anywhere else on earth.

DOROTHY FRANCES GURNEY, *FROM 'GOD'S GARDEN'*

Heavenly Herbs

*'I know that if odour were visible,
as colour is, I'd see the summer
garden aureoled in rainbow clouds.'*

ROBERT BRIDGES, *THE TESTAMENT OF BEAUTY*

Your precious herb plants will thrive when a fistful of grit is added into the hole in which they are planted. The grit helps with drainage and keeps the foliage dry, reducing the risk of rot.

GARDEN LORE...

An old wives' tale goes that if you slip borage into your lover's drink it will give them the courage to propose marriage.

Give your mint an extra strong flavour by planting chamomile next to it.

If you find that you are particularly tasty to gnats, rub some fresh mint leaves over your skin.

Make your own cold cure by gathering fresh rosemary from the garden and plunging it into a bowl of boiling water. Inhale the infusion.

────────

'Those herbs which perfume the air most delightfully, not passed by as the rest, but being trodden upon and crushed, are three; that is, burnet, wild thyme and watermints. Therefore, you are to set whole alleys of them, to have the pleasure when you walk or tread.'

FRANCIS BACON, *ESSAYS, CIVIL AND MORAL*

────────

Mint and lemon grow apace in the garden – it's best to plant these in pots and sink the containers into the soil to prevent these particular herbs from hogging the kitchen garden.

GARDEN LORE...

Never plant the same type of herb in the same spot twice or the second will wither and fail.

Make your own mint sauce for a Sunday roast – simply pick two large handfuls of the freshest leaves from your mint plants, wash and chop them into tiny pieces and place in a serving bowl. Add 4 tablespoons of white wine vinegar, 4 tablespoons of hot water and one tablespoon of caster sugar. Allow to cool and serve.

Dill and coriander are best planted in a shady spot as they can quickly go to seed when placed in direct sunlight. Harvest the leaves regularly to encourage healthy new growth.

Flies hate chives, so keep a pot of them on your kitchen windowsill to discourage the airborne pests from entering the home.

GARDEN LORE...

An old wives' tale goes that parsley should never be given away, as misfortune will be sure to follow.

Basil originally came from India and is therefore happiest in a humid climate. Grow these plants either indoors or in a sheltered spot with the top half of a plastic drinks bottle covering it for protection from the elements.

'As for the garden of mint, the very smell of it alone recovers and refreshes our spirits, as the taste stirs up our appetite for meat.'

PLINY THE ELDER

Pick herbs just as they are coming into flower for maximum flavour. The best time of day to harvest them is in the morning, before the sun is at its height, so that the natural oils of the plant haven't been dried out.

In the same way that chamomile is used to soothe a person who is out of sorts, it can also be used to give an ailing plant a lift when it is planted beside it.

Sage plants need to be replaced every few years, as the older they are, the less flavour they have – take cuttings in order to grow new plants.

Store your dried herbs in airtight jars in a cool, dark place. They should remain fresh for up to two years.

Comfrey has long been known for its medicinal purposes and it works equally well as a fertiliser and natural cleanser to your plants when grown in the garden, providing a rich source of potassium, nitrogen and phosphorus.

Make lavender bath bags – pick sprigs of lavender just before the plant comes into flower for maximum scent, tie together and leave to dry in a warm place away from sunlight for a couple of weeks. Place the lavender in squares of muslin, chop the stalks down if necessary and tie the bundles with twine. Make a loop so that a bag can be hung underneath the hot tap when the bath is running to scent the water.

'As is the garden such is the gardener. A man's nature runs either to herbs or weeds.'

FRANCIS BACON

GARDEN LORE...

Basil is regarded as sacred in India and it is believed that burying the dead with a sprig of basil will ensure their safe passage to heaven.

Make a herbal vinegar salad dressing by gathering herbs from the garden – rosemary, basil, parsley, fennel or coriander, for example. Tie the herbs together and leave to dry in a warm place. When the herbs are completely dry, find a tall, clear glass bottle, sterilise it – by cleaning the bottle with boiling water and allowing it to air dry – and add the herbs. Fill the bottle with warmed white wine vinegar, making sure that the herbs are completely covered, as exposed herbs tend to go mouldy. Place the lid on the bottle and leave to infuse for a couple of months. If you are giving this as a present, you might like to sieve the mixture to remove the herbs and place some fresh stems in the bottle for decoration.

A few sprigs of herbs scattered onto the charcoal at a barbecue will give a lovely aroma while waiting for the food to cook.

Thyme loves to grow around rocks and paving stones, so make a feature of it by having some decorative tiles for them to grow around in your kitchen garden.

Home cooks will find that growing a selection of herbs in a window box outside the kitchen window is very handy – that sprig of rosemary or parsley for the finishing touch to your culinary creations will never be far from reach.

After a hard day's toil in the garden, treat yourself to a mojito made with home-grown mint. Pick eight mint leaves, rinse them, and crush with a mortar and pestle, add to a glass with one part freshly squeezed lime juice and two parts white rum. Fill the glass with sparkling water and ice with sugar to taste and a sprig of mint for decoration.

Parsley thrives in the shade but can take a while to germinate, so it's best to buy plants from the garden centre and replant these into your herb garden. Snip off the leaves regularly with scissors — but don't be too scissor-happy, as excess cutting can destroy the plant.

Though a life of retreat offers various joys,
None, I think, will compare with the time one employs
In the study of herbs, or in striving to gain
Some practical knowledge of nature's domain.
Get a garden! What kind you may get matters not.

WALAFRID STRABO, 'HORTALUS' OR 'THE LITTLE GARDEN'

Gardens in the Air

Be still. The Hanging Gardens were a dream
That over Persian roses flew to kiss.

TRUMBULL STICKNEY, 'BE STILL...'

Roof gardens and balconies are often exposed to cold and damaging winds. The higher the balcony the greater problem strong wind is likely to be. To grow tender and exotic plants, provide a screen that will filter the wind without causing turbulent eddies.

If your balcony or roof garden has little floor space, incorporate upward-growing plants, fountains, hanging baskets and trellises to maximise vertical space. Screens and trellises can be cloaked with wispy, tall grasses, climbers or bamboo plants for privacy without blocking out valuable light.

Balconies conjure up romantic connotations, but remember if you decide to add trellising below it you may find that it is not just your Romeo who ascends the wall!

GARDEN LORE...

In bygone Italy, basil was considered to be a symbol of love and women would grow pots of it on their balconies to attract a suitor.

If your balcony has an overhang which prevents rain from reaching your plants, get a professional to install a gutter pipe along it, running down to a container to provide a continually fresh supply of rainwater that you can dip into with a watering can to refresh your plants.

'There is more pleasure in making a garden than in contemplating a paradise.'

ANNE SCOTT-JAMES

If you are purchasing expensive pot plants from the garden centre for your balcony or roof garden, give the container a sharp tap and carefully lift out the plant to examine its roots. Make sure they are white and wispy and growing well; you don't want to be paying out for a large amount of compost with a small, under-established plant.

It's important not to overload your roof garden or balcony, so use lightweight containers such as plastic or wicker, or go for lookalikes rather than real terracotta or zinc.

Remember: a few well-placed large pots can give a much more spacious feel to your balcony than dozens of tiny ones.

'If I'm ever reborn, I want to be a gardener – there's too much to do in one lifetime!'

KARL FÖRSTER

A recipe for long-term potting mixture goes as follows: one part grit, one part loam, one part leaf mould and two parts compost from the garden. Give the plants a 'comfrey feed' once in a while for an extra boost of nutrients. Make your own comfrey feed by piling comfrey leaves into a water-tight container and covering them with water. Leave it in a sunny spot and hold your nose when you open it in a few weeks' time! Add the liquid fertiliser to your potted plants and watch them grow.

If you decide to defy the wind and have a potted tree on your roof garden or balcony, here's a tip: heavy stones or rocks placed around the trunk can help to counterbalance the tree's weight and keep it upright.

For a long-lasting hanging basket, line the base with an old jumper (be sure that you will not want to wear it again!) and cut it to fit the basket. Make holes in the jumper where you would like your plants to go. Add a small amount of compost and some slow-release fertiliser granules. Push the plants through the underside of the basket and through the holes that you have made. Fill with compost and plant some trailing plants on the top of the basket such as fuchsias and geraniums. Once you have finished planting, give it a good water and hang it up.

To protect wicker baskets from the elements, give them a few coats of yacht varnish.

When buying plants for your roof terrace, consider low-growing ones that will withstand strong winds or those that move with the wind rather than resisting it, such as lavender and mallow. If you have a bit of shelter, climbing roses and grapevines will flourish on trellising with a bit of extra maintenance.

Make sure any furniture that you use in your roof garden is put away or secured in some way when not in use – you don't want a re-enactment of the great storm in *The Wizard of Oz* every time there are strong gusts!

If you are 'potting on', a clever tip is to put the smaller pot inside the bigger one and fill around it with soil so that the space left when you lift the small pot out is the right size for the plant.

The rose upon my balcony
the morning air perfuming,
Was leafless all the winter time
and pining for the spring.

WILLIAM MAKEPEACE THACKERAY,
'THE ROSE UPON MY BALCONY'

Down to Earth

'After forking muck all day, the après-compost hot bath is doubly rewarding.'

NIGEL COLBORN

SOIL

Find out your garden's soil type by picking some up and rubbing it between your finger and thumb. If the soil blows away then it is sandy. If it clumps together then it is clay. Both soil types have their advantages. If you have recently moved to a new area, why not have a walk round and see what is growing successfully in your neighbours' gardens?

Healthy soil should be home to a community of earthworms, centipedes and beetles, which help to aerate the soil and break down organic matter. Attract them to your garden by maintaining the pH level between 6.0 and 7.0, and keeping the soil well fertilised.

GARDEN LORE...

An old farmers' proverb goes that if you till the soil in April showers, you will have neither fruit nor flowers.

'To forget how to dig the earth and tend the soil is to forget ourselves.'

MAHATMA GANDHI

Spread sheep's wool around if you have clay soil – it helps to break it down, improving aeration and draining the soil. It also adds nutrients to the soil as it breaks down.

Only dig the soil when it's dry. A simple test is to see if mud is sticking to your boots as you garden – if this is the case, then it is too wet. The best way to dig the soil is to have the spade upright and to perform a chopping motion with the blade – always bend your knees when digging as it puts less strain on your back.

Use plenty of compost on sandy soil as it will improve the texture by filling in the holes between the tiny stones of which sand is composed. This will also increase its ability to hold water and nutrients.

When you stop for a tea break, give your grass some too! Open a tea bag and sprinkle the tea on your lawn – it makes a great natural fertiliser.

'If you think "Hoe hoe" is a laughing matter, you're no gardener.'

HERBERT PROCHNOW

Decomposed leather is rich in nutrients, so don't throw your old leather shoes away — bury them in the garden.

Laying a bulky organic mulch over the ground will encourage an open, well-drained soil surface and stop moss from growing over your soil.

If you have loam soil in your garden consider yourself very fortunate indeed; this perfect blend of sand and clay is very fertile and will support almost any kind of plant, including those which need moist soil, such as prairie wildflowers and bramble fruits.

If you come across many stones whilst turning, chances are you have chalk soil; often overlaying limestone bedrock, this soil loves crab apple, juniper, silver cup and maiden pink, but isn't so kind to acid-loving plants such as rhododendrons.

Clay soil makes a good base for growing trees, but it goes rock-solid when dry so it will need a good soaking with the hose before you attempt to dig it. Regular hoeing and manure will help retain its moisture in hot weather.

'The longer I live the greater is my respect and affection for manure.'

ELIZABETH VON ARNIM

With a warm and gritty texture, sandy soil is easy to identify; use it to plant Mediterranean herbs, lavender, marigold and daisies, which all love a warmer soil temperature.

If there is a river close to your garden, you will probably have silty soil, which is smooth, soapy and heavier than sand; this soil retains water well and is rich in nutrients so is ideal for a healthy lawn.

'My wife's a water sign. I'm an earth sign. Together we make mud.'

RODNEY DANGERFIELD

COMPOST

Compost can be used to balance out both acidic and alkaline soils so it is an ideal way to improve your soil, whatever type you have been blessed with. It is made when leaves, grass clippings, vegetable and fruit scraps, woodchips, straw and small twigs are combined and allowed to break down into a soil-like texture. Use it instead of commercial fertilisers wherever possible, as not only is it cheaper and organic, and any produce from your garden will taste better, but there is far less risk to small creatures, family pets and children.

'Earth knows no desolation. She smells regeneration in the moist breath of decay.'

GEORGE MEREDITH

Ensure your compost material breaks down efficiently by placing your bin or heap in a sunny/semi-shaded spot for maximum heat, and on soil for good drainage and easy access to beneficial bacteria and insects.

Your compost pile should be no smaller than one cubic metre. At this size the pile will generate enough heat to decompose while still allowing for sufficient airflow. Invest in a compost thermometer from your local garden centre, and remember that the ideal temperature for effective composting is between 55 and 65°C. This heat is achieved when enzymes effectively break down the molecules of the composting material.

To give your compost a kick start, throw a few shovelfuls of old manure, alfalfa or blood meal over it, and then add some more during the process as an extra boost. This will provide the compost with plenty of bacteria, giving the microbes energy to break down material.

Worms are invaluable for composting and a home-made wormery is great fun for small children. Use a large, clean aquarium or glass container and add a centimetre of sand to the base; next add a few centimetres of moist soil and another layer of sand and continue with the stripy effect until your jar is two-thirds full. Add the worms and some leaves and vegetable peelings and screw the lid on, making sure that there are some holes in the top. Leave the wormery in a cool, dark place (such as a corner of the shed) and check on it after a couple of weeks to see how the peelings have been broken down. Relocate the worms to your compost heap so they can get to work!

'all the vegetable mould over the whole country has passed many times through, and will again pass many times through, the intestinal canals of worms.'

CHARLES DARWIN, *THE FORMATION OF VEGETABLE MOULD, THROUGH THE ACTION OF WORMS, WITH OBSERVATIONS ON THEIR HABITS*

It is a good idea to keep track of how many 'green' and 'brown' items you add to your compost pile as this will affect the rate at which the material breaks down. One part green to two parts brown should be the perfect mix.

Everyday waste 'green' items include: vegetable peelings, dead flowers, tea bags, grass cuttings, old fruit, coffee grounds and filter paper.

Everyday waste 'brown' items include: cardboard, newspaper, cotton wool, egg shells (you'll need to crush these first), string, ash, straw/hay, dry leaves and hedge clippings.

Have a layer of twigs and branches at the bottom of your compost heap to provide vertical airflow though the material; on top of this mix in your 'browns' and 'greens' with thin layers of grass mowings, dead flowers, manure and straw. Sheep manure is probably the richest source of nutrients, just ahead of horse manure. Chances are you can probably find both for free if you know a friendly farmer or horse owner.

'*The ground must touch a man before he can amount to much.*'

ABRAHAM LINCOLN

Don't add these to your compost pile: charcoal or coal ashes, which contain high amounts of sulphur; cat or dog droppings, which might contain disease; and perennial weeds, which will only put weeds back into your soil once you spread your compost – uprooted annual weeds are fine for composting but only before they set seed. And unless you fancy attracting rats to your garden, avoid adding eggs or meat to the mix.

'To turn ordinary clothes into garden clothes, simply mix with compost.'

GUY BROWNING

Weed-free and pesticide-free grass clippings bring nitrogen to your compost — be sure to mix them in well to avoid smells and to get the maximum benefit from the grass.

If you want your compost heap to remain active during winter, keep it in a place that gets lots of sunlight, or insulate the sides with hay to keep the compost warm.

Turn your compost pile every two weeks for fast results. The finished compost should look and smell like rich, dark soil.

Compost can be made in six to eight weeks, or it can take a year or more. The more effort you put in, the quicker you get compost.

Your compost pile should be moist all the way through so be sure to wet each layer and add water every time you add to it.

May God grant thee
Enough sun to warm the earth,
Enough rain to make things grow,
A good strong back,
A wide-brimmed hat,
And a good sharp goose-neck hoe

RALPH EMERSON PURKHISER, 'GARDENER'S BLESSING'

Add birch leaves to your compost heap – they disinfect the soil and prevent the spread of diseases from flies.

When distributing the first results of your compost spread it in an area that needs the most attention and has the worst soil. This will show you the effectiveness of your compost.

Apply compost to your soil two to four weeks before new planting as this gives the compost time to integrate with the soil.

Plants benefit most from compost when it is mixed thoroughly with the soil to a depth of six inches, as plants growing in a layer of pure compost will struggle to send roots down below it into the soil.

Algae, seaweed and lake weed are good additions to your compost pile but remember to wash off the salt water before adding them.

Do not leave a finished compost pile standing unprotected as it will lose nutrients. Special breathable compost cover sheets can be found at any garden centre.

Once you have nibbled all the sweetcorn off a corn cob, chop up the stalk and throw it onto the compost pile.

Don't throw your fingernail clippings in the bin – they make another welcome addition to the compost pile.

'Did you see the pictures of the moon? They must have the same gardener I have.'

HARRY HERSHFIELD

Sowing the Seeds

'We may think we are nurturing our garden but of course it's our garden that is really nurturing us.'

JENNY UGLOW

If the label on a plant says it needs sun, it means it requires direct sunlight for eight hours a day. If it says shade, that means less than four hours of sunlight a day. 'Part sun' means four to six hours a day.

GARDEN LORE...

In the Middle Ages, farmers had all sorts of rituals when it came to planting crops for the coming year. One of the more outlandish of these was to leap high into the air astride a garden fork so that the harvest would grow tall and strong!

Sow very small seeds by mixing them with a little sand in a sugar shaker or plastic yoghurt pot with holes in the bottom; this ensures that they are evenly distributed.

When sowing seeds that you have not tried before sow some in a separate pot to use as a reference. This way, when the seeds start to grow, you will know what to look for and will not confuse them with weeds.

*'All the flowers of all the tomorrows
are in the seeds of today.'*

INDIAN PROVERB

Make a shallow trench for your seeds by laying down a broom handle and walking along it to press it down firmly.

It is always better to sow seeds on a waxing moon. This is because the lunar rhythms that affect the earth's atmosphere make it more likely to rain immediately after a full or new moon. (A new moon is when the moon is directly between the Earth and the Sun and is barely visible in the sky.)

Sow seeds between 2 p.m. and 4 p.m. so that the temperature-sensitive phase of the germination process is completed at night when soil temperatures are lower; this way you will get a better rate of germination.

Cardboard egg boxes are great to use instead of seed trays – use one compartment for each seed. You can then plant the box straight into the ground, as the cardboard will decompose.

Don't throw out those empty seed packets yet; they will provide valuable information about plant height and spacing.

Seeds with hard outer casings, such as cannas and black-seeded varieties of sweet peas, need a little help to germinate so try these tricks before planting: soak them in warm water for 24 hours to soften them up, or make a small cut in the seed with a sharp knife to help the fleshy part to push through. If the seeds are too small for this, line a jar with sandpaper (rough side facing inwards), place the seeds inside and shake the jar until the seeds become scratched and weakened.

GARDEN LORE...

Farmers in medieval times believed that sowing seeds whilst naked would yield a better harvest. This is partly due to the weather needing to be reasonably mild for successful germination and therefore temperate enough to briefly go without clothes.

When planting bulbs in the garden, first plant them inside a flowerpot at approximately three times their depth and then bury the pot as the pot can be more easily lifted once the bulbs have grown and finished flowering.

'A garden is a grand teacher. It teaches patience and careful watchfulness; it teaches industry and thrift; above all it teaches entire trust.'

GERTRUDE JEKYLL

Give your bulbs a good squeeze before planting. If the bulbs feel soft, chances are they are harbouring bulb fly larvae. Don't despair – a 60-second turn in the microwave at 750 W will kill all the bugs, leaving you free to plant healthy bulbs.

Don't throw away your squeezy lemon juice container after Pancake Day – keep it in the greenhouse and refill with water for watering fragile seedlings drop by drop without damaging them.

Seed saving is something that can be done at the end of summer and can save quite a bit of money in the long run. Instead of deadheading all your flowers, when you notice a flower head beginning to dry out, place a paper bag over it, secure it with a length of twine, cut the stem and hang the bag in a warm place indoors. Shake the bag once the head is completely dried out to release the seeds. Save the seeds in small envelopes and be sure to mark them with the flower's name ready to be sown early next year.

'My garden of flowers is also my garden of thoughts and dreams. The thoughts grow as freely as the flowers, and the dreams are as beautiful.'

ABRAM L. URBAN

The Green, Green Grass

'The original Garden of Eden could not have had such turf as one sees in England.'

CHARLES DUDLEY WARNER,
MY SUMMER IN A GARDEN

Refrigerate grass seeds for a couple of days before sowing to encourage more vigorous growth.

Pick a fine day with only light winds to sow your grass seed. The soil needs to be dry.

To ensure an evenly sown lawn, divide the area into equal shares and allocate the same amount of seed for each square. Lightly rake the area to cover the seed.

Ornamental grasses are a great solution if you have little time for regular garden maintenance or if you fancy a Zen garden with gravel rather than lawn but still want year-round green. As well as only requiring a trim in the spring they are also rarely dined upon by slugs.

Keep birds away from the grass seed and, of course, your other precious plants, by making a garland of shiny objects. Thread foil, CDs, old cutlery and bottle tops onto garden string and hang from trees and hedges so that they flap in the wind.

'The kind of grass I've got in the garden lies down under the mower, and pops up again as soon as it's passed.'

BASIL BOOTHROYD

GARDEN LORE...

According to American folklore, if a dog eats grass in the morning then it will almost certainly rain by nightfall.

The mowing year begins in March, when the grass begins to grow with vigour, and ends in October, when growth stops. Aim to mow the lawn once a week in spring and autumn, but you may need to mow twice a week in the height of summer. Mow only when the grass is dry.

'A perfect summer day is when the sun is shining, the breeze is blowing, the birds are singing and the lawnmower is broken.'

JAMES DENT

Molehills are a real blot on the landscape. A humane method of sending moles packing is to plant glass bottles (without lids on) into the molehills with the top of the bottle showing so that the noise of the wind travels through their tunnels, encouraging them to move to a more peaceful location.

Aim to remove weeds without weed killer, as using it can be harmful to pets, by digging the offenders out with a knife or narrow-bladed trowel. Try to dig out the roots to prevent regrowth but without disturbing the lawn too much.

Give your lawn a makeover in the spring by first raking over the area and then pricking the soil with a pitchfork. Get some sand and sprinkle it all over the lawn, then brush the sand into the holes with a broom. Finally, sprinkle grass seed over the area, making sure that bare patches are covered, and water. This will give your lawn a much needed wake-up call after the long winter.

Daffodils scattered across a lawn look beautiful in the spring but they can make it difficult to cut the grass, which causes the grass to deteriorate. Plant the bulbs in drifts to minimise the area of lawn affected.

'I believe a leaf of grass is no less than the journey-work of the stars.'

WALT WHITMAN

Try not to walk on a frost-covered lawn; not only is it slippery and dangerous, but it will damage the brittle grass and leave unsightly bare patches of earth.

Fallen autumn leaves look beautiful but they need to be raked off the lawn to prevent the grass from yellowing underneath.

Water your lawn during dry spells in spring and summer. You may need to water it as much as twice a week in the height of summer. Make your own sprinkler by recycling an old garden hose. Once it has sprung a few leaks, simply make a few more holes with a sharp nail and *voilà*! The best time to water your lawn is in the early morning – watering in the heat of the day will make the water evaporate too quickly and could damage the grass, while watering in the evening may make the grass excessively damp overnight, which could cause lawn diseases to form.

> 'There's one good thing about
> snow – it makes your lawn look
> as nice as your neighbour's.'
>
> CLYDE MOORE

Weed 'em and Reap

'What is a weed? A plant whose virtues have not yet been discovered.'

RALPH WALDO EMERSON

Don't throw away those dandelion leaves; they are rich in vitamins A, C and K, and also contain iron, potassium and calcium. Pick the freshest leaves for a great addition to a salad. Don't forget to wash them first!

If daisies are thriving in your garden, it means the soil is too acidic.

Burdock roots, once cleaned and chopped, can be added to stir fries.

'I would rather do a good hour's work weeding than write two pages of my best; nothing is interesting as weeding. I went crazy over the outdoor work, and at last had to confine myself to the house, or literature must have gone by the board.'

ROBERT LOUIS STEVENSON

Clover is good for the lawn as it boosts the nitrogen in the soil and it can be mown. It also attracts honey bees into your garden in the spring and summer and prevents more harmful and less attractive weeds from taking up the space.

Stinging nettles are very unpopular in a garden but rather than consigning them to the compost heap, try making a very tasty soup with them. Use gloves to pick them, and keep your gloves on when washing and picking the leaves off the stalks. To make the soup, melt a knob of butter and fry two roughly chopped onions along with half a kilo of peeled and sliced potatoes. Add a litre of vegetable stock, bring to the boil and leave to simmer for 10 minutes. Add the nettle leaves and cook for a further 10 minutes. Blend the mixture with 100 ml of single cream, then add lemon juice and pepper to taste before serving.

GARDEN LORE...

Finding a four-leaf clover is a well-known good luck omen. According to legend, this superstition is believed to have come about when Eve plucked one of these so that a piece of paradise would remain with her when she was banished from the Garden of Eden.

Make 'friendly' weed killer for your lawn by mixing two parts boiling water with one part malt vinegar (the type that you sprinkle on your fish and chips). Decant the liquid into an airtight bottle and administer with a spray-bottle on a sunny day for best results.

'The philosopher who said that work well done never needs doing over never weeded a garden.'

RAY D. EVERSON

Yarrow is another unpopular weed that is often removed, but it is very beneficial for companion planting because not only does it repel pests and attract good insects, but it improves the condition of the soil.

The daisy is a happy flower,
And comes in early spring,
And brings with it the sunny hour
When bees are on the wing.

JOHN CLARE, 'THE DAISY'

Try not to use chemical fertilisers on your lawn as these can be harmful to animals and people. A simple home-made alternative is to spread used coffee grounds over the lawn which gives the grass a good nutrient boost – the positive effects of which can be seen within a couple of weeks.

GARDEN LORE...

Daisies are believed to foretell the strength of your suitor's love, hence the popular ritual of pulling the petals off one by one and saying 'He loves me, he loves me not'.

For a healthy snack, pick a few fresh leaves from the following: yellow dock, lamb's quarters, dandelion, cress and sorrel, and fry them with chopped garlic and olive oil, then add lemon juice and seasoning to taste. These 'weeds' have greater nutritional value than spinach.

An infusion of dandelion petals is a great tonic for indigestion, and a brew from the roots of the plant makes a potent diuretic.

'I always think of my sins when I weed. They grow apace in the same way and are harder still to get rid of.'

HELENA RUTHERFORD ELY, *A WOMAN'S HARDY GARDEN*

The Fruits of
Your Labours

---

*'In an orchard there should be enough
to eat, enough to lay up, enough to be
stolen and enough to rot on the ground.'*

JAMES BOSWELL

Ensure a bumper apple harvest in autumn by scattering cooled bonfire ash around the bases of your fruit trees in the spring.

Peach trees can be affected by leaf curl, which can severely deplete the leaves and fruit and in some cases destroy the tree. To prevent this, hang moth balls from the branches.

GARDEN LORE...

Those who believe in fairies say that drinking elderberry wine will help you see the fairy folk!

Apples are irresistible to wasps. The best way to keep them from spoiling your harvest is to hang a couple of jam jars containing sugared water on the branches to catch them in.

Gather your windfall fruit and cook up some delicious chutney. Remove the stones of a kilo of plums, and the cores of the same quantity of apples. Blend or finely chop with the same quantities of tomatoes and onions, before placing all the fruit and veg into a large saucepan with half a teaspoon each of cayenne pepper, mixed spice, mace and 500 g of sultanas. Add 500 ml of vinegar and bring to the boil. When the fruit has softened, stir in 500 g of sugar. Continue simmering for two hours until the mixture is thick. When cooled decant into sterilised jars. To sterilise jars, wash in hot, soapy water, then rinse well. Place the jars, still wet, on a baking sheet and place in the oven at 140°C/275°F/gas mark 1 until dry.

What wondrous life is this I lead
Ripe apples drop about my head;
The luscious clusters of the vine
Upon my mouth do crush their wine;
The nectarine and curious peach
Into my hands themselves do reach;
Stumbling on melons, as I pass,
Ensnared with flowers, I fall on grass.

ANDREW MARVELL, 'THE GARDEN'

Make your own apple sauce with four fat cooking apples plucked straight from the tree. Peel, core and quarter them and place in a large pot with a few strips of peel and the juice of a lemon, half a cinnamon stick, half a cup of equal parts brown and white sugar (i.e. a quarter cup of each) and a cup of water. Simmer for 30 minutes, then remove from the heat and take out the peel and cinnamon and mash the mixture before serving.

GARDEN LORE...

Make a toast when planting your apple trees and bathe its roots in cider to promote longevity and a healthy harvest.

A grapevine makes a beautiful, natural covering to a pergola. Have the pergola in a sunny spot with rich compost and good drainage – water liberally in the evenings.

'Even if I knew that tomorrow the world would go to pieces, I would still plant my apple tree.'

MARTIN LUTHER

If you want to grow your own fruit trees but lack the space in your garden, there are many types that thrive in containers, including peaches, cherries, lemons, olives, limes, figs and apples. Wrap the trunks of any warm-climate trees in fleece or bring them indoors during the winter months to protect them from frost damage.

Make toffee apples for an autumn party. First, place the fruit in a large bowl and cover with boiling water from the kettle to remove their waxy coating, if they are shop-bought. Pat them dry with a tea towel, twist off the stalks and firmly push a wooden skewer into each. Pour 400 g of golden caster sugar and 100 ml of water into a saucepan and simmer for 5 minutes until the sugar has dissolved. Stir in one teaspoon of vinegar and 4 tablespoons of golden syrup. Using a sugar thermometer, boil to 140°C. The final mixture should harden instantly when poured into cold water; if it is still runny, it isn't done yet. Carefully dip the apples into the hot toffee mixture by holding the end of the skewer, and leave to cool on a piece of baking parchment.

Apple trees need a companion to cross-pollinate, and preferably a different variety but with the same bloom time, so unless your neighbour has an apple tree make sure you plant more than one for an abundant harvest.

Make dried fruit – it will mean that you can enjoy your harvest for many months to come. Chop a variety of fruits into bite-size pieces. Dip the pieces into lemon juice before you begin the drying process, so they don't turn brown. Skewer whole grapes and cherries as this will ventilate the skins. Evenly space the fruit on a baking tray, and place in a cool oven at about 50°C/120°F. It will take several hours for the pieces to dry out completely. Once they have a nice, chewy texture, they are ready to eat. Store your dried fruit in an airtight container.

If your garden slopes at all, plant your fruit trees uphill, away from trouble spots for cold winds and frost.

Fig trees thrive when their roots are restricted, so they make ideal potted trees.

Make a pomander; it's a natural air freshener that will fill your home with a wonderful citrus scent. An orange works best. Push large-headed cloves into the skin of the fruit at random intervals so that only the heads are protruding – wear gloves when doing this as they can be quite sharp. Roll your creation in a mixture of orange juice, cinnamon and nutmeg powder and wrap it in tissue paper or cheese cloth and leave to dry in an airing cupboard for a few weeks. By this time, the orange should have dried out. Wrap a ribbon around it and hang it up.

Position pear trees against a wall or sheltered spot to give them a bit of shelter from the frosts in spring, as they blossom early.

GARDEN LORE...

If the apple trees bloom in April, the yield will be good, but if they don't blossom until May, the harvest will be poor.

To make a sweet, sticky strawberry jam, first warm 850 g of caster sugar on a baking tray in a preheated oven at 120°C/275°F/gas mark 1 for about 10 minutes. Crush 500 g of hulled strawberries in a large bowl with a masher or fork. When the sugar is warm and runny, stir it in with the strawberries and leave for 4 hours at room temperature, stirring occasionally. Mix in one sachet of pectin crystals or half a bottle of the liquid form, along with 3 tablespoons of lemon juice. Ladle the mixture into sterilised jars, cover and leave to set at room temperature for around 3 hours. If it has difficulty setting by this point, add another tablespoon of lemon juice. The mixture should be fully set and ready to eat in 24 hours.

Lay straw around your strawberry plants to keep the fruits off the ground and protect them from grey mould, which can completely destroy the crop.

For a traditional apple and blackberry crumble, sieve 340 g plain flour into a large bowl and mix with 170 g unsalted butter to a crumbly consistency. Sprinkle a little rum over the peeled chunks of six cooking apples and 250 g of blackberries in an oven dish. Cover the fruit with the crumble mixture and cook in a preheated oven at 180°C/350°F/gas mark 4 for 35–40 minutes until golden brown. Test the apples with a knife to see that they have cooked all the way through.

Aim to keep the stalks attached to your cherries when harvesting, as this will help maintain their freshness.

'The sun, with all those planets revolving around it and dependent on it, can still ripen a bunch of grapes as if it had nothing else in the universe to do.'

GALILEO

Flower Power

'What a desolate place would be a world without a flower! It would be a face without a smile, a feast without a welcome.'

A. J. BALFOUR

Newly purchased flowers are best planted in the late evening or on a cloudy day. Their chance of survival is far greater if they are planted in the rain rather than in sunny conditions.

If you have an abundant supply of pesticide-free red or hot-pink roses, you can make rose-petal jam. Gather approximately 60 rose petals and cut away the light-coloured base of the petals, as this can make the jam bitter. Place a kilogram of jam sugar and a litre of water in a saucepan and bring to the boil, stirring constantly. Add in the petals and simmer for 20 minutes – stir occasionally. Add a teaspoon of citric acid and stir for a further 10 minutes – you should notice the jam gelling; if not, stir for a little longer. Pour the mixture into sterilised jam jars and seal. Once cooled, the jam can be served with scones or ice cream.

Daffodils signify the arrival of spring and there are many varieties to choose from. Try some of the smaller narcissus varieties as they keep their shape and are less likely to topple over in strong winds.

'Earth laughs in flowers.'

RALPH WALDO EMERSON

If you live in a new-build house and your garden is not yet established, buy several packets of annuals, such as marigolds and petunias, and sow them in the spring for a dazzling floral display that will provide plenty of flowers to decorate the home as well.

An arrangement of blue and orange flowers can have a soothing effect on nerves and anxiety.

GARDEN LORE...

A British tradition states that it is bad luck to give a bunch of red and white flowers to someone who is ill in hospital: it is said that the colours together symbolise blood and bandages and, therefore, ill health.

When creating a rose arch, avoid using climbing roses as these can appear scraggly and scant on flowers. It's far better to obtain a variety of rambling rose that has sufficient growth around the base, and leave the climbing roses for the wall.

Bury banana skins just below the surface of the soil surrounding your roses. They rot quickly, releasing calcium, magnesium, potassium and other beneficial nutrients.

Plant daffodil bulbs before the end of October; cheer them up by mixing dry mustard with fertiliser when you plant the bulbs – they will turn an even brighter yellow!

To encourage hollyhocks to grow, give them some beer, as they thrive on the yeast.

'There should be beds of roses, banks of roses, bowers of roses, hedges of roses, edgings of roses, baskets of roses, vistas and alleys of roses.'

SAMUEL REYNOLDS HOLE, *A BOOK ABOUT ROSES*

When giving flowers as a gift, consider the connotations; here are a few of the most popular varieties and their meanings:

- Clover – Good luck!
- Cornflower – You are elegant and refined.
- Daffodil – Wishing you loved me.
- Hyacinth – Forgive me.
- Red rose – I love you.
- Foxglove – I don't trust you.
- Yellow poppy – Wishing you wealth and success.
- Primrose – I can't live without you.
- Narcissus – You love yourself too much!

Planting a few foxgloves in the garden will stimulate growth in surrounding plants and fend off diseases.

———————

*'You have heard it said that flowers
only flourish rightly in the garden
of someone who loves them. I know
you would like that to be true; and
would think it a pleasant magic if you
could flush your flowers into brighter
bloom by a kind look upon them.'*

JOHN RUSKIN, FROM HIS LECTURES 'SESAME AND LILIES'

———————

Buy your spring plants once the weather has warmed up, as a sudden move from a sheltered garden centre or nursery to a cold garden plot can kill the plants stone dead.

Train climbing roses to grow horizontally as this will encourage the growth and blossom of buds across the branches rather than just the tips.

'There are no flowers that never fade,
Yet here are the chrysanthemums,
Still blooming in winter.'

YUAN HUNG-TAO

If you are lucky enough to have a wooded area in your garden, plant a swathe of bluebells. They are best planted 'in the green', which is when the bulbs have sprouted green leaves, in February and March.

'Flowers always make people better, happier and more helpful; they are sunshine, food and medicine for the soul.'

LUTHER BURBANK

Some roses, with a bit of tender care, will flower throughout the summer months; these include the Bengal, the tea and noisette varieties, amongst others. Plant late-flowering clematis with your roses, so that you will continue to have blooms after the roses have finished their display.

GARDEN LORE...

An old superstition states that a bunch of violets worn around the neck will protect the wearer from drunkenness, and a common saying goes that if you dream of violets you advance in life.

Pick flowers in the early morning or late evening before the buds have opened. This is when they will be at their freshest.

Flower petals make a colourful and nutritious addition to salads. Marigold, nasturtium, day lily, gladiolus and honeysuckle petals are some great edible flowers. It's important that the flowers you use have not been sprayed with any kind of chemicals. Pick the flowers when you are about to add them to your dish and wash them in cold, salted water to remove any bugs, dry the petals and serve.

Crocuses like shade so plant them around tree bases or below hedges.

Ah, Sun-flower! weary of time,
Who countest the steps of the Sun:
Seeking after that sweet golden clime,
Where the traveller's journey is done.

WILLIAM BLAKE, 'SUNFLOWER'

Sunflower seeds will thrive if planted around your compost heap, and when they grow tall they'll hide the unsightly heap. Just make sure you leave an opening to access the compost without damaging the flowers!

Tulips are sun lovers so plant them in a sunny spot with good drainage. They should be planted in the autumn with your daffodils. Never pair them with lilies as they suffer from the same diseases and if one becomes infected they will pass the disease on to the other.

Don't place manure near to tulips during the growing process, as it is too strong for them. Instead, use well-drained compost to nourish the bulbs before they flower.

Large clumps of shop-bought perennials, such as begonias and sweet william, can be instantly separated into smaller plants, creating a more abundant display.

'A half-moon, dusky gold, was sinking behind the black sycamore at the end of the garden, making the sky dull purple with its glow. Nearer, a dim white fence of lilies went across the garden, and the air all round seemed to stir with scent... He went across the beds of pinks, whose keen perfume came sharply across the rocking, heavy scent of the lilies, and stood alongside the white barrier of flowers. They flagged all loose, as if they were panting. The scent made him drunk.'

D. H. LAWRENCE, SONS AND LOVERS

Protecting Your Paradise

'A thorn defends the rose, harming only those who would steal the blossom.'

CHINESE PROVERB

Sweet-smelling lavender not only attracts beautiful butterflies into your garden but also deters slugs, snails and aphids, so plant liberally.

Prevent frost damage to your precious plants in winter by spraying them with cold water in the evening. This will generate enough heat during evaporation to protect from frost.

The next time you boil the kettle, sprinkle any leftover water on your cabbage crop to kill off those pesky cabbage worms.

Plant onions amongst the other vegetables in your garden to deter rabbits – the marauding rodents also dislike foxgloves, so plant a few nearby.

GARDEN LORE...

An old wives' tale has it that burying horse hair will trap unwanted bugs in the soil and prick them to death.

'The ant is knowing and wise, but he doesn't know enough to take a vacation.'

CLARENCE DAY

Deter the local cat population by liberally seasoning your garden with pepper.

Plant basil amongst your tomato plants to repel unwanted visitors. Chives grown amongst rose bushes deter ants and other pests.

Scare the pigeons away by painting some plastic bottles red and upending them on sticks near your plants.

Repel slugs and snails from your plants by spreading either crushed eggshells or used coffee grounds around infested areas. The caffeine in the coffee dries the slugs out as it makes them produce excess slime.

'If I outrun 'em in the yard, how come they beat me to the chard?'

ALLEN KLEIN ON SNAILS

If grasshoppers appear to be eating their way through your garden, plant coriander around the perimeter – the little creatures seem to hate the smell.

Red spider mites cause leaves to become discoloured; remove these by watering the affected plants daily with cold water.

Slugs and earwigs are both partial to beer, so if your garden is under siege, simply fill a few shallow dishes with beer and watch the pests congregate!

Keep your cat away from your prize plants and young seedlings by planting a container of catmint elsewhere in the garden — cats find this irresistible.

GARDEN LORE...

In ancient Greece farmers believed that when faced with a mouse infestation they should write polite letters to the rodents suggesting alternative accommodation!

Cat owners who love tulips are in luck, as the mice that normally like to feast on tulips will be frightened away by your feline friend.

Protect your new bulbs from hungry squirrels and other small creatures by adding a layer of chicken wire to the surface of the planted area.

Using plants as a deterrent is an excellent way of improving the security of your home. Human intruders will find prickly shrubbery and thorny climbing roses very off-putting when grown on garden walls, along fences, boundaries and surrounding windows. Holly, blackberry bushes, roses, and cacti are just some of the plants you might want to try, as these are attractive as well as good deterrents. If your fence or wall isn't very tall, add a trellis with a thorny climbing plant, or surround both sides with thick, spiky hedging.

Evict those earwigs from your dahlias by placing an upturned flowerpot on a stick and filling it with tissue. Position it near to your flowers and you will soon find that the little critters have relocated to this luxurious new abode.

Make garlic water to spray on your new plants as this will deter slugs. Crush a couple of garlic cloves, add them to a saucepan containing a litre of water and bring it to the boil. Strain the liquid and pour it into a glass bottle with an airtight lid. When watering your seedlings, add a tablespoon of the garlic water for every 4–5 litres of water in your watering can. Make sure to repeat this after wet weather so that the plants remain protected.

'Did you know that ducks are natural predators of slugs? As the old saying goes, if you have too many slugs the chances are you have a deficiency of ducks.'

MICHAEL POWELL, *THE ACCIDENTAL GARDENER*

The Vegetable Patch

'To get the best results you must talk to your vegetables.'

PRINCE CHARLES

Peas and beans make happy vegetable patch companions. Ensure that the rows run north to south, since the sun moves from east to west, giving the plants maximum sunlight.

The larger the vegetable seed, the deeper it should be sown. Roughly speaking, smaller seeds such as onions, lettuces and carrots should be sown about half an inch deep, whereas larger seeds such as cabbages should be one inch deep and beans two inches deep.

To maximise your vegetable plot, plant two vegetable crops in the same furrow by mixing a fast-growing vegetable, such as lettuce, with a slow-growing one, such as parsnip or carrot. Alternatively, you can keep sowing the same type of vegetable every few weeks; wait for the first crop to be at the thinning stage and sow again.

Treat your carrot seeds to fresh manure mixed with some old coffee grounds so they grow straight and tall.

Harvest onion bulbs when the tops have fallen over. Remove them from the ground and clean away any soil before storing them in a cool, dry place.

GARDEN LORE...

Human hair placed in the trench when planting beans will ensure a rich harvest.

Rather than planting canes to support your peas, a more decorative option is to gather branches or strong twigs and stick them into the ground at roughly half-metre intervals for your plants to climb.

Remember potatoes and tomatoes both come from the nightshade family, so don't plant them one after the other. And no matter how small your vegetable patch, you should be aware of the importance of crop rotation because if you grow the same crops year on year you will get a build-up of diseases specific to those crops. The simple rule is not to grow the same crop for two years running.

Make tomato salsa dip from your own prize crop. Pick three large tomatoes, peel and chop them and place in a bowl. Add an onion, a small green pepper, one mild green chilli and two cloves of garlic, all finely chopped. Mix in a tablespoon of olive oil, 3 tablespoons of lime juice and a handful of finely chopped fresh coriander leaves. Stir the ingredients and then cover the bowl and place it in the fridge for at least half an hour so that the flavours can mingle. Serve with tortilla chips and sangria!

'In order to live off a garden, you practically have to live in it.'

FRANK McKINNEY HUBBARD

Old guttering is great for irrigating the vegetable patch. Drill small holes along the guttering, lay it alongside your row of vegetables and pour some water into one end.

If you don't own a cloche to protect your precious potato seedlings from frost, use sheets of newspaper weighted down with stones — it may look unsightly but you can remove the coverings in the morning.

Sow a variety of lettuce seedlings in late March–July, such as romaine and leaf, in rows roughly 15 cm apart – many types of lettuce can be grown closely together to produce baby leaves for salads. Pick the leaves as soon as they are a few inches long – the plants will regrow several times so that you can 'cut and come again'.

If you haven't tried growing salad vegetables before, rocket is foolproof for starting out as slugs despise it!

Grow onions and carrots together as the smell from the onions acts as a deterrent to carrot fly. Another method for reducing the risk of these pests destroying your crop is to thin the foliage in the evenings and do any harvesting at this time of day.

If using a container to plant salad vegetables, make sure there are plenty of holes for drainage; fill the container with a mixture of nutrient-laden manure and fine compost. Leave a lip of at least 5 cm to allow for plant growth.

'*Lettuce is like conversation: it must be fresh and crisp, and so sparkling that you scarcely notice the bitter in it.*'

CHARLES DUDLEY WARNER

To make crispy vegetable pakoras, sift 75 g of chickpea flour into a bowl with half a teaspoon each of coriander, turmeric and chilli powder, one teaspoon of salt and two crushed garlic cloves. Pour in 175 ml water and mix to a smooth batter-like consistency. In a large saucepan heat enough oil for deep-frying to 190°C; then coat florets of vegetables of your choosing in the batter and fry until golden brown (around 4–5 minutes). Drain off any excess oil on kitchen roll when cooked.

Garlic is a difficult plant to propagate and you should always grow from a plant rather than from part of a bulb from the supermarket, because the shop-bought garlic can carry disease. When it starts to grow, it is important that you remove the flower buds so all the plant's energy is concentrated on forming the bulb.

'A Gard'ner's Work is never at an end; it begins with the Year, and continues to the next.'

JOHN EVELYN, *KALENDARIUM HORTENSE* OR *THE GARD'NERS ALMANAC*

After you have hollowed out your Halloween pumpkin and carved a scary face to ward off evil spirits, make pumpkin pie with the leftover flesh. Remove the seeds, cut the flesh into chunks (you will need roughly 550 g for a 30 cm tart tin) and microwave it in a bowl on high (approximately 850 W) for 15 minutes. When it has softened, transfer it to a colander to cool and drain. Meanwhile roll out some pastry and line a tart tin with it, leaving an overhang, then bake blind until it becomes golden brown. For the filling, blend together the pumpkin with two eggs, 175 g sugar, 140 ml double cream, a teaspoon each of cinnamon, allspice and ginger, and a little grated nutmeg until the mixture has a smooth consistency. Use it to fill the pastry case and bake for an hour at 180°C/350°F/gas mark 4, then serve with whipped cream.

'Dilettante gardeners love the spring and summer; real gardeners also love the winter.'

ANNE SCOTT-JAMES, *DOWN TO EARTH*

For a tasty squash soup, finely chop an onion and a clove of garlic to be lightly sautéed in a little oil in a large pan for 5 minutes. Cut a hole in the top of the squash (you can use whichever type you wish), remove the seeds, peel and chop up the fleshy part. Add this to the pan along with a teaspoon of turmeric and sauté for another 5 minutes. Pour in a litre of stock (of your choice) and leave to simmer for an hour, stirring occasionally. Then purée the mixture in a blender. It's easy to freeze and reheat if there's quite a lot of it.

Increase the size of your artichoke heads by making two incisions in the fully developed stalk just below the head and inserting two criss-crossing matchsticks.

Grate a couple of large courgettes and toss them in a bowl with a little salt, pepper, lemon juice, honey, poppy seeds and crushed garlic to make a refreshing, zesty salad.

'It's obvious that carrots are good for your eyesight. Have you ever seen a rabbit wearing glasses?'

STEVE McQUEEN

Seeing the Wood for the Trees

'He who plants a tree, plants a hope.'

LUCY LARCOM

The best time to plant trees is during their dormant period from late autumn to early spring.

If you live in a city or near a busy road where the air is more polluted, tolerant trees such as maple, horse chestnut, alder, silver birch or poplar are the best varieties.

Ever fancied trying your hand at topiary? You can buy a ready-made chicken wire topiary frame from a garden centre – there are endless shapes to choose from, including animals, spheres and teacups. Place the frame over a shrub – the most common varieties for small topiary are box and yew – tug the branches through the wire, and trim them back so they just hide the wire from view. Regular pruning will encourage the plant to grow around the wiring.

GARDEN LORE...

Silver maples will show the lining of their leaves before a storm.

Water young trees regularly, especially those on semi-dwarfing or dwarfing root stocks, to ensure that the root system becomes well established.

Use a stem guard to protect your saplings from foraging animals.

Check the growth rate of trees before purchasing, and make sure you leave enough space between each tree for the fully grown version to sit comfortably without having to compete for water or sunlight.

Plant trees with interesting barks to give year-round colour and texture to the garden. Some great varieties include Himalayan birch, which has a bright white trunk, and flowering cherry, which has a mahogany-red trunk.

The most important time to prune trees is late winter before you see any signs of new growth. Prune off damaged limbs as well as branches that grow too close to the main branches.

'Trees are much like human beings and enjoy each other's company. Only a few love to be alone.'

JENS JENSEN

Unless you have a very large garden, it is best to steer clear of poplar and willow as they have widespread and fast-growing root systems which can cause serious damage to foundations and drainage systems.

To make pine needle tea, place two large handfuls of fresh, washed pine needles into a small saucepan, cover with water and bring to the boil, then allow to simmer for 10 minutes. Extract the needles with a draining spoon and steep the brew for 5 minutes, filter, pour into cups and add sugar to taste.

'There were other trees in the garden, and one of the things which made the place look strangest and loveliest was that climbing roses had run all over them and swung down long tendrils which made light swaying curtains, and here and there they had caught at each other or at a far-reaching branch and had crept from one tree to another and made lovely bridges of themselves.'

FRANCES HODGSON BURNETT, *THE SECRET GARDEN*

Plant 'ever-greys' among your evergreens for added visual interest in the winter months – these are silver-leafed evergreens such as lavender, santolina and artemesia.

A willow bower makes a charming spot to shelter from rain or sun in your garden. Use the edge of a spade or piece of wood to mark a circle in the ground that will be the base of the bower. Plant about eight long whips of willow into the earth, spaced evenly along the circle line, leaving an opening for the entrance to the bower; you will just need to push the willow deep into the ground (water the ground first if it is hard). Tie the tops of the whips together in opposite pairs, and then for the difficult bit – insert two more willow whips per gap and draw them across diagonally to create a criss-cross pattern. Fasten all overlaps securely and wait for your willow bower to fill out with leaves.

The ideal time to plant out shrubs is in the autumn, as the mix of sunny and rainy days provides perfect conditions for the roots to grow and establish themselves before the onset of winter.

'I frequently tramped eight or ten miles through the deepest snow to keep an appointment with a beech-tree, or a yellow birch, or an old acquaintance among the pines.'

HENRY DAVID THOREAU

Make hardwood cuttings from any deciduous shrubs before winter sets in. Cut 20-cm lengths from the pencil-thin stems and plant in a partially shady spot, leaving the top half of the stem visible. Make sure you water them in dry weather and label them. It takes about a year for the roots to emerge, and then you can either pot them on or replant them elsewhere in the garden.

Give your garden that stately home feel with a scaled-down version of a tree-lined avenue — two rows of attractive potted dwarf trees or neatly trimmed shrubs will add a touch of class to your driveway.

GARDEN LORE...

According to an ancient British tradition, the secret to eternal youth is to carry an acorn about your person at all times – this is because oak trees are strong and live to a ripe old age.

I think that I shall never see
A poem as lovely as a tree.

JOYCE KILMER, 'TREES'

Spice Up Your Life

'It is a golden maxim to cultivate the garden of the nose, and the eyes will take care of themselves.'

ROBERT LOUIS STEVENSON

Grow your own mustard seeds in the same way as cress. Use an old yoghurt pot or margarine tub, fill it with damp kitchen roll and add a damp layer of cotton wool on top. Sprinkle the mustard seeds over the cotton wool and gently press them in. Leave it in a light and dry place and they should begin sprouting after a week. The mustard crop can be used as a flavouring in salads and many other dishes.

Marigolds are easy to grow and can be used as an alternative to expensive saffron – they have a light, delicate flavour and their petals can be used to colour food.

GARDEN LORE...

Plant olive stones amongst young garlic plants to make the produce sweeter.

'When gardeners garden, it is not just the plants that grow, but the gardeners themselves.'

KEN DRUSE

Cardamom will flourish if you grow it in a very warm spot indoors – ideally your bathroom. The leaves are flavoursome and ideal for wrapping around vegetables, rice or fish while they cook.

Fenugreek leaves have the flavour of fresh peas and make a delicious addition to salad, and the seeds are used as a culinary spice. Sow seeds in mid-spring just below the soil's surface; it will take only a few days for them to germinate.

When planting ginger root, soak the tubers overnight to stimulate growth – especially if you are using shop-bought ginger as it may have been treated with a growth retardant – and plant them in a pot just below the soil surface with the buds facing upwards. Keep the pot indoors as ginger thrives in warm climates.

Coriander and turmeric need a warm and sunny environment to grow, so if you don't have a greenhouse, grow them on a windowsill indoors that gets lots of light in the day. Turmeric gives that distinctive golden yellow colour to spicy dishes, while both coriander seeds and leaves can be used in cooking.

Ginger tea is a great natural remedy for nausea, colds and indigestion. Peel a 5-cm piece of root ginger and slice thinly. Bring a litre of fresh water to the boil in a pan and add the ginger. Cover and simmer for 15 minutes, strain and pour into cups to serve.

Dried chillies strung together look very decorative in the kitchen and can make a great present for the chilli addict in your life. Use cayenne, fiesta and serenade varieties. Run a needle and thread through the thickest part of the stems and hang your garland to dry in the sunshine for three weeks – preferably outside as they can leak liquid during the drying process. Alternatively, you can speed up the drying process in the oven. Wearing gloves, spread the chillies out on a baking tray and put them in for two hours at 160°C/325°F/gas mark 3, turning them over after an hour.

GARDEN LORE...

In southern India people believe that hanging a few chilli peppers with a lemon over the threshold of their home will protect the occupants from evil spirits.

To make a tasty chilli pepper relish, peel and finely chop 2 onions, a cucumber, 2 cooking apples and 12 dried chillies and mix together in a bowl. Tightly pack the mixture in sterilised jars. Make up a mixture of half a pint of white vinegar, 225 g of caster sugar and a tablespoon of table salt, stir until the sugar has dissolved and pour the liquid into the jars so that the vegetables are completely covered. Screw on the lids and leave to marinade for three weeks before eating.

Tools of
the Trade

'Other people's tools work only in other people's gardens.'

ARTHUR BLOCH, MURPHY'S LAW AND OTHER REASONS WHY THINGS GO WRONG

When buying tools, be sure to handle them first to check that they feel comfortable and aren't too heavy, especially the ones that you will use on a daily basis, such as a trowel and secateurs.

Keep tools rust free and good as new by having an oily rag to hand in the garden shed and wiping them after use at the end of the day.

'What a man needs in gardening is a cast-iron back, with a hinge in it.'

CHARLES DUDLEY WARNER

Use an old pair of tights to store and hang bulbs or onions in your shed.

Grow your own bamboo canes. Bamboo looks lovely in the garden, and can be harvested in autumn and dried in a cool, dry place ready for use when planting runner beans or sweet peas.

GARDEN LORE...

One superstition goes that you should never carry a hoe into the house as misfortune is sure to follow. To appease any evil spirits you must retrace your steps backwards and out of the same door that you entered.

You don't need to spend money on labels and tags to keep track of your plants; stones make great natural markers that blend into the landscape. Look for flat, smooth stones, wash and dry well, then label each one using permanent ink or paint, if you're feeling creative.

Remember not to throw away old ice lolly sticks because they make good plant labels too.

You can spend a bundle on a seed-planting device called a dibber. It's basically a blunt, pointed stick used for 'drilling' a hole into the soil to plant seeds, seedlings and bulbs. Or you can use a trusty old screwdriver to perform the same function for free.

When you finish a loaf of packaged bread, don't throw away the tie – they are perfect for securing the leggy stems of tomatoes, pole beans, peas and other climbing plants to their stakes.

'To a gardener there is nothing more exasperating than a hose that just isn't long enough.'

CECIL ROBERTS

Organise all your plants and seedlings and keep track of herbs by painting the collars of clay pots with stripes of chalkboard paint. Once they are dry, you can pot up your plants and label them with chalk. When you reuse the pot, you can simply wipe the chalk off and write on a new label.

Be gentle on newly planted seeds; use an ordinary sieve or pasta strainer to lightly dust them with soil when first sowing, as a layer too thick can prevent them from germinating properly.

Setting an egg-timer can be a helpful reminder when watering plants or using a sprinkler on the lawn – over-watering can cause plants to rot.

————

'There is no gardening without humility. Nature is constantly sending even its oldest scholars to the bottom of the class for some egregious blunder.'

ALFRED AUSTIN

————

Store your prized tools away from ground level – hang them up if you can. A surprising amount of moisture can come up through shed and garage floors and cause rusting.

Use antibacterial wipes when cleaning your pruners between cuts to keep your plants healthy and disease-free.

To keep your metal tools free of rust, fill an old bucket with builder's sand mixed with a litre of motor oil and use it to store the tool blades in.

Don't get rid of empty plastic milk cartons; give them a new lease of life as watering cans. Simply pierce holes in the sides around the base and partially bury them amongst your flowers. Fill them as needed, and your plants will have a steady, gradual supply of water.

Fill an old hot water bottle with polystyrene chips for a waterproof and wipe-clean knee cushion to make those long gardening jobs a little more comfortable.

———————

'We might as well abandon our spades and pitchforks as pretend that nature is everything and art nothing.'

JAMES SHIRLEY HIBBERD

———————

Water, Water, Everywhere

'Water is the driver of nature.'

LEONARDO DA VINCI

When choosing the ideal spot for your pond, remember that pond plant life, such as lilies, will need sunlight to bloom, so don't pick a shady spot. The leaves of trees such as oak, yew, laburnum, elder and poplar are poisonous and could harm any pond life if they fall in the water, so set the pond a good distance away if you have any of these in your garden.

Allow small birds, butterflies, frogs and insects to enjoy your pond by placing a few large, flat stones at the water's edge for them to rest upon.

───────────

'How fair is a garden amid the toils and passions of existence.'

BENJAMIN DISRAELI, *SYBIL*

───────────

A fountain or waterfall in the pond will prevent the water from stagnating, but bear in mind that water lilies will not cope well with the constant disruption, so plant them at the opposite end of the pool.

Plants that are best for small ponds include parrot's feather and willow moss, which act as vital oxygenators. For the edges, have a few well-spaced rushes, such as spike and corkscrew. For floating plants, try water lettuce and water hyacinth and, of course, water lily – even the smallest ponds can accommodate certain varieties of lily such as pygmy and dwarf white.

Larger birds can be a real nuisance when you have a pond, especially ones with a penchant for small fish. Aside from purchasing plastic bird decoys or devices that emit high-pitched sounds, a simple solution is to cover the pond with netting, making sure it is securely weighted down around the perimeter so that small birds and animals don't become trapped underneath.

GARDEN LORE...

People in the Middle Ages used to carry the dried corpse of a frog around their necks in a small bag made of silk, as it was believed that this would protect them from experiencing fits.

If you suspect frost overnight, leave a plastic ball bobbing in the pond to stop it from completely freezing over. Remove the ball in the morning (you may need to use some hot water for this) and you will have an air hole for any pond dwellers. If you are caught out by the frost, pour some hot water into a plastic bottle and lay it onto the ice to thaw gradually.

─────────────

'There were the smoothest lawns in the world stretching down to the edge of the liquid slowness and making, where the water touched them, a line as even as the rim of a champagne glass... The place was a garden of delight.'

HENRY JAMES, *ENGLISH HOURS*

─────────────

Don't throw away any algae that you remove from the pond – add it to the compost pile.

If you are stocking your pond with goldfish, the best time to do this is from the beginning of spring to the end of summer. Try not to overpopulate the pond and remember that some varieties of goldfish can grow to upwards of 15 cm. The general rule for fish ponds is that they must have a minimum depth of 50 cm and it is best to aerate the pond with an airstone or pump. Goldfish are very hardy and can live happily in temperatures ranging from freezing to 30°C. Feed them with pellets and make sure there is plenty of weed for them to nibble on.

'A pool is the eye of the garden in whose candid depths is mirrored its advancing grace.'

LOUISE BEBE WILDER

Lay a Little Egg for Me

'Regard it as just as desirable to build a chicken house as to build a cathedral.'

FRANK LLOYD WRIGHT

The ideal hen house has both a secure sleeping area sheltered from the elements and an enclosed outside area for them to exercise and feed. Base the size of your house on the number of birds you intend to have; each bird will need at least a square foot.

Roosting perches made of strong branches are more natural to chickens and will help them settle in to their new home. They should be about 5 cm wide and set 50 cm off the ground.

Chicken feed is very attractive to rodents, so make sure that it is stored away in a metal container and be careful not to put too much feed out in the first place. Also, collect eggs as often as possible, as these are another food source for unwelcome rats. Be on the alert for damage to the hen house and patch up any holes as soon as you see them.

To keep things interesting for your chickens, hang a cabbage on some thick string so that they can peck at it from the ground, or equally hang some old shiny CDs high up to catch the light to grab their attention. You could place logs in their run for them to scratch at or perch on, or even create a ramp and higher level.

You'll need one nesting box for every three hens. Line them with straw to prevent egg damage, and don't place them higher than the perches so that they are easily accessible. If you are building nesting boxes, be sure to make the roof (of the nesting box) slanted or otherwise it's likely the chickens will decide to roost there instead and inevitably make a huge mess!

GARDEN LORE...

The name 'foxglove' is derived from a legend which claims that evil fairies gave a fox the flower petals to put onto his toes so that he could sneak into the chicken house without being heard!

Eggs are the perfect comfort food and are incredibly versatile. Here's how to make an egg custard tart. First make and bake a basic sweet pastry case in a 25-cm flan case. To make the filling, pour 480 ml of whipping cream and the scrapings from a vanilla pod into a saucepan and bring to the boil. Whisk 6 egg yolks and 70 g of caster sugar in a large bowl, then pour the cream into the bowl and stir. Spoon the mixture into the pastry case and top it off with some grated nutmeg. Bake in the middle of the oven at 180°C/350°F/gas mark 4 for half an hour or until the mixture has set. Place the tart onto a plate and serve.

'Noise proves nothing. Often a hen who has merely laid an egg cackles as if she had laid an asteroid.'

MARK TWAIN

Don't be concerned if new chickens don't perch for the first few weeks; it takes a little time for them to settle in.

With the exception of some featherless ex-battery hens, chickens are quite capable of keeping themselves warm; they will perch near to each other and fluff their feathers. If you want to give a new home to ex-battery hens it might be best to wait for spring when the weather is a bit warmer, so they will have the chance to develop a thicker plume before winter sets in.

GARDEN LORE...

Do not bring eggs into your home after nightfall as it is considered bad luck.

Those who have a vegetable patch – be warned! If chickens are allowed to wander free in the garden (or they escape into the garden) they will not know the difference between things they can eat and what you'd rather they didn't. Be sure to securely fence off any produce you don't want to lose.

Protect your chickens by returning them to the security of their house and pen when you go out, even if it's only for an hour. Foxes and other predators do not always wait for nightfall to go looking for food.

Freshly laid eggs are best for making poached eggs. The difference in taste is very noticeable compared with shop-bought eggs, which can be a month old or more.

Although they are fairly easy to care for, it's advisable to confirm with your local vet any vaccinations your fowl might need. You can tell a healthy chicken by its brightly coloured, perky comb. Their most common ailments, lice and dust mites, can be solved with a regular dusting of treatment powder.

'Then there was a farmer who got rid of his incubator because he'd had it over six months and it hadn't laid even one egg.'

DOUG SANDERSON

Get the Buzz

*'The hum of bees is the
voice of the garden.'*

ELIZABETH LAWRENCE

Bees need access to a fresh supply of water. If there is no water source nearby you can create one by lining a large dish with gravel and regularly topping it up with tap water, making sure that the water level lies just below the gravel. If you have a new colony, add a couple of teaspoons of sugar to keep up their reserves as it takes the bees a while to establish their pollen-hunting territories.

*The pedigree of honey
Does not concern the bee;
A clover, any time, to him,
Is aristocracy.*

EMILY DICKINSON , 'POEMS V'

The equipment required for beekeeping includes a large cardboard box with a tight-fitting lid, hives with foundation comb, smokers, secateurs, sack, gloves and veils. Nowadays, ready-to-use beekeeping equipment is available on the market. You can purchase bee equipment rather than building it on your own. Assemble it as per the manufacturer's directions. It is always advisable to use new equipment for beekeeping because there is a risk of pathogen contamination and/or spreading of diseases when using second-hand apparatus.

Planting a few hemlock plants around the hive can protect it from harsh, cold winds.

GARDEN LORE...

Some are suspicious about a bee entering the home as they believe it signifies the imminent arrival of a visitor. Kill the bee and the visitor will be an unpleasant one.

Anywhere that is prone to loud noise, frequent passers-by or strong winds will create stress for the colony, so try to situate them in a quiet, secluded spot that will still be easily accessible by the time you come to harvest the honey.

Avoid placing the hive in full sunlight as this will make the colony work on overdrive trying to regulate the temperature during summer. Equally a situation too dark could make the bees listless and expose the hive to damp. It's best to give them dappled light, with the entrance facing south-east to catch the morning sun.

The queen bee can survive between two and five years, whilst the workers (female bees) live for one to four months and the male drones only 40–50 days. But don't worry, with new larvae hatching all the time their short life span shouldn't interfere with their population numbers.

Having an empty second hive located close by will give the bees a place to swarm to if they become overpopulated.

Since they use up a lot of energy in the first year becoming a full-sized colony, bees will need all of their honey to survive the winter. You can start collecting honey in the late summer to early autumn of the second year.

If you suffer from hay fever, try eating locally produced honey (within a 30-km radius of your home) – some sufferers say it works wonders.

Package bees and a nucleus colony are excellent bee sources for beginners. Collecting bee swarms and transferring bees from trees are not recommended for beginners, as this can be difficult and dangerous. When purchasing a bee source, ensure that the bees are free of mites and diseases.

What Does the Bee Do?

What does the bee do?
Bring home honey.
What does father do?
Bring home money.
And what does mother do?
Lay out the money.
And what does baby do?
Eat up the honey.

CHRISTINA ROSSETTI

Make honey fudge by mixing 170 g of margarine, 3 beaten eggs, 142 g caster sugar, 170 g of self-raising flour and a tablespoon of honey. Bake the mixture in a shallow tin for 20 minutes in a moderate oven. Allow to cool and cut into squares and serve.

If you have a fruit orchard, locate the hive amongst the trees so that the honey they make has a hint of fruit flavouring. If you have a few acres of land you might want to try to alter the flavour of your honey by planting purple lavender for a lightweight, sweet honey, red roses and morning glories for a slightly heavier consistency, and marigolds or dandelions for a really thick, full-bodied variety. Unfortunately this won't work for smaller gardens as bees tend to fly up to 8 km from their hive to gather pollen.

GARDEN LORE...

An ancient superstition decrees that mouth ulcers can be cured with a dab of honey. This isn't as outlandish as it first sounds because honey is well known for its antibiotic properties.

Sweet is the garden, white with bloom,
Heavy with honey, drenched with scent.

KATHARINE TYAN HINKSON, 'LOVE
CONTENT', *A LOVER'S BREAST-KNOT*

The best times to start beekeeping are late spring or early summer. Bee veils should be worn while handling bees in order to protect the face and neck. Leather gloves or thick gloves of white or a dark colour are preferable to protect from bee stings. You should provide water in a dish near the apiary; otherwise bees may use any water source present in the nearby area. At times of food scarcity or shortage of nectar, you can provide sugar syrup to the bee colony. Overcrowding of bees in the hive should be checked, in order to prevent swarming or splitting of the colony. You can divide the colony if the number of bees increases extensively.

The amount of honey you can take will vary from year to year; to give you an idea, the average colony will need about 15 kg to get through winter — anything more than that is yours for the taking.

Even if you don't intend to keep your own hive, you can still attract honeybees and bumblebees into your garden to pollinate the plants; they love flowering vegetables and fruits such as cherries, strawberries, blackberries, raspberries, apples, pears, peaches, cucumbers, squash and pumpkins, to name a few. They also particularly like nectar-producing plants in these colours: blue, violet, purple, white and yellow.

Around the House

*'I'd rather have roses on my table
than diamonds on my neck.'*

EMMA GOLDMAN

To keep your house plants in optimum condition, simply pinch off any damaged or discoloured leaves and petals as they appear. And since a build-up of dust can inhibit growth, keep them clean by wiping them with a piece of damp cotton wool regularly. A mild organic soap spray can protect against mealy bug and other pests that feed on sap.

Use plant pots with a reservoir in the bottom if you do not have the time to water regularly. The soil can then soak up the moisture from the reserves as needed.

Make your own fragrant pot pourri by picking rosemary, lavender, rose petals and lemon balm leaves. Place the rose petals in a dry container and stir them every three days. Tie the remaining cuttings together with twine and hang upside down to dry indoors. After two weeks, break up the dried cuttings, stir them into the petals and distribute the pot pourri in bowls to bring the smell of the garden into your home.

GARDEN LORE...

The hanging up of mistletoe branches indoors comes from a medieval tradition, and is believed to bring good luck and fertility to the occupants of the home.

Put pinpricks in a tulip's stem just below the flower head to prevent them from drooping too quickly.

Poppies will last a little longer if you singe the base of their stems with a lighter before arranging them.

Cut lily stems at an angle and store them up to their necks in a bucket of water for an hour before arranging them.

To revive droopy flowers, drop an aspirin or two into the water; a copper coin will work equally well.

'To pick a flower is so much more satisfying than just observing it, or photographing it... So in later years, I have grown in my garden as many flowers as possible for children to pick.'

ANNE SCOTT-JAMES

Create some attractive and low-maintenance window boxes by planting a selection of evergreens, which will give you a year-round display. Plant small conifers and miniature holly bushes – these plants are slow growing but can be transplanted to the garden once they get too big for the box.

Be experimental when it comes to making floral displays; a jug of pussy willow or catkin stems looks really striking, as does a combination of hedgerow finds, such as rosehip, hawthorn and rowan, laden with autumn berries.

Kitchens and bathrooms are the best place to keep house plants that like high humidity. If the soil dries out quickly it's a sure sign that the air is too dry. To increase humidity levels try grouping plants together, or misting them with a morning water spray – use rainwater or water that has been boiled and cooled to prevent leaving white residue over the leaves.

'A flowerless room is a soulless room, to my way of thinking; but even one solitary little vase of a living flower may redeem it.'

VITA SACKVILLE-WEST

When you go on holiday, if you don't have someone to come round and water your plants, try putting smaller potted plants in the bath on an old towel soaked with water. For larger plants it would be best to get some slow-release plant food from a garden centre.

Keep aloe vera, cutleaf philodendron, hydrangea and golden pathos out of reach of children and pets. If ingested they can cause a range of unpleasant reactions including vomiting and fits, and can even be fatal.

Cover the soil of potted plants with large flat stones or a piece of needlepoint canvas cut to shape so pets aren't tempted to dig them up.

A catmint plant could lure your cat away from other house plants if purposely placed in an easy-to-reach area.

If your bathroom is quite large, you might consider including a tall potted plant such as bamboo. It will thrive in the humid atmosphere. And for well-lit bathrooms, ferns, orchids and azaleas can be a very pretty addition, whereas bathrooms with less light can house peace lilies, heart-leaf philodendron and African violets.

Plants that will help to improve the air quality of your home by filtering out toxins, pollutants and carbon dioxide include peace lily, gerbera daisies, bamboo palm, English ivy and chrysanthemums.

If you are going away for a few days, fill a plastic jug with water and put one end of a piece of cotton rope in the jug and the other end in the plant pot. The rope will act as a wick, taking water from the jug to the plants and keeping them happy while you are away.

———————————

'He who is born with a silver spoon in his mouth is generally considered a fortunate person, but his good fortune is small compared to that of the happy mortal who enters this world with a passion for flowers in his soul.'

CELIA THAXTER

———————————

Creatures Great and Small

'I value my garden more for being full of blackbirds than cherries, and very frankly give them fruit for their songs.'

JOSEPH ADDISON

If you have a large patch of lawn that receives a lot of sunlight, plant a wildflower meadow. It is low maintenance and provides food and shelter for many insects and small mammals. A spring-flowering meadow could contain plants such as cowslips, buttercups, violets and fritillaries, whilst a summer-flowering meadow could contain scabious, campions, harebells and ox-eye daisies.

Primroses not only symbolise the start of spring but they also attract finches into the garden.

If you have a dark corner where nothing much grows, how about creating a pile of rotting logs to attract rare insects such as stag beetles? Adding leaf litter will encourage hibernating hedgehogs and toads to use the habitat as a safe hideaway.

'Poor indeed is the garden in which birds find no homes.'

ABRAM L. URBAN

Put up nest boxes around the garden – on trees, trellises and fencing. Make the boxes and entry holes different sizes to encourage tits, robins and even owls to nest there.

Rockeries and dry-stone walls make secure habitats for amphibious creatures, such as frogs and newts. Make sure there are plenty of gaps between the stones to encourage creatures to take up residence.

GARDEN LORE...

If you are plagued by 'wild' cats in the garden, they will disperse with the smoke of bitter almonds and rue!

Ladybirds consume around 5,000 aphids in a lifetime, making them a great natural form of pest control. A bundle of cow parsley hung in a sheltered nook of a tree will attract these insects into your garden.

'The toad has indeed no superior as a destroyer of noxious insects, and he possesses no bad habits and is entirely inoffensive himself, every owner of a garden should treat him with utmost hospitality.'

CELIA THAXTER, *AN ISLAND GARDEN*

Place bird feeders near foliage to give visiting birds protection from the elements and any predators, and choose locations that can be viewed from the house.

A supply of fat balls will help sustain visiting garden birds through the winter months. To make your own, get a combination of wild bird seed, nuts, porridge oats and kitchen scraps (such as stale bread, cheese or cake crumbs), then mix two parts of these dry ingredients with one part melted lard or suet in a bowl. Distribute the mixture into plastic containers, such as yoghurt pots, and thread twine through the containers and the centre of the balls. Leave the containers overnight in the fridge. Cut the containers away and tie knots into one end of the pieces of twine before hanging them from a tree.

Leave a few old and broken clay pots around the perimeter of the garden, as they make great homes for frogs and toads.

Don't be too diligent about clearing away leaf litter, as it provides a valuable habitat and food source for many types of insects.

Encourage bats to feed in your garden by growing night-blooming flowers such as moonflower and yucca — these will attract moths and other nocturnal insects for the bats to feast on.

If you buy netted fat balls, be sure to remove the fat balls from the nets before suspending them in your garden, as small birds can get their feet trapped in the netting.

Make the birds in your garden their very own Christmas tree — festoon one of your trees with pieces of coconut, apple and cheese on strings and home-made fat balls on ribbons. You could even top it off with a star made of straw. You will be rewarded with a fantastic display of bird life throughout the festive season.

Bats have dwindled in numbers in recent years, but you can help in the conservation of these fascinating creatures by installing a bat box in your garden. For an easy guide to making a well-insulated and secure bat box, visit the Bat Trust website. Position the box high up away from predators and be careful to leave the bats undisturbed; it is illegal to handle or disturb the creatures without a licence.

Oh! pleasant, pleasant were the days,
The time, when, in our childish plays,
My sister Emmeline and I
Together chased the butterfly!
A very hunter did I rush
Upon the prey: – with leaps and springs
I followed on from brake to bush;
But she, God love her, feared to brush
The dust from off its wings.

WILLIAM WORDSWORTH, FROM 'TO A BUTTERFLY'

Finishing Touches

'*A garden is the best alternative therapy.*'

GERMAINE GREER

If your garden doesn't get much sunlight, paint your fences a pale colour and add reflective surfaces, such as polished planters or mirrors, or a water feature.

Create wacky and interesting containers for your plants by drilling adequate drainage holes into anything from wheelbarrows and old bathtubs to disused plastic toys and kettles.

Sandpits are great fun for the kids to play but are notoriously messy. You can minimise mess by positioning yours next to a patio so that you can sweep up the sand with a broom and return it to the sandpit. Use 'silver sand' as it has a fine texture and will not stain or turn into a sodden mess when it rains. When the kids grow out of it, convert your sandpit into a herb garden, or even a water feature, by adding a waterproof lining.

GARDEN LORE...

Old wives believe that you will have good luck all the year through if the first spring butterfly you see is white.

A tree swing can really make the most of an outside living space. To hang a swing safely, you must choose a branch or beam that is at least 20 cm in diameter and 3 m above the ground. Oak trees are the ideal size and shape to accommodate a swing but any large tree with a strong, level branch will also work well. Cedar and redwood are the best types of wood to use for a swing seat as they are both durable and naturally rot-resistant.

Plant some solar-powered lights into your borders and hang some lanterns or chains of lights from trees or hedges. Not only will a lit garden look lovely from your windows at night but it also means you can utilise the garden in the evenings for socialising and relaxing, or catch up on some weeding!

If garden gnomes are your thing, why not add a personal touch by getting a paint-your-own-gnome kit from your local garden centre?

Wind chimes can act as a deterrent, keeping birds away from your fruit trees, and they also produce a lovely calming sound in a gentle breeze. Be careful not to place them in too windy a spot though, or you'll find that the soothing chimes become an irritating clanging.

Old-fashioned milk churns, cow bells, cart wheels and farm tools can make interesting outdoor features. Hang them up, lean them up against a brick wall or position them in a flowerbed.

If you have a long pathway, remember that large sculptures placed in sight at the end of it will draw people onwards.

Polish up an old oak barrel from a garden centre or reclamation yard to use as a seat, side table or even for planting things in.

Finally, enjoy your garden, have picnics, play games, enjoy a drink outside and take time to appreciate all your hard work!

'Live each day as if it were your last, and garden as though you will live forever.'

ANONYMOUS

Useful Websites

www.bbc.co.uk/gardening
Includes an A–Z of pests, lawns, house plants, organic gardening, ponds… pretty much everything.

www.bbcgoodfood.com
Find recipes for delicious pickles, jams and chutneys, as well as food for many calendar events.

www.bbka.org.uk
If you're looking for beekeeping courses in the UK, check out a thorough index of associations and local courses here, as well as news of upcoming beekeepers' conventions.

www.compostdirect.com
Online suppliers of landscaping materials: barks, mulches, soil improvers, green waste bags and other garden goodness.

www.farmersmarket.net
An easy-to-navigate directory of all the UK's inspected and certified farmers' markets.

www.farmshop.uk.com
Find your local farm shop, selling local produce here.

www.gardenadvice.co.uk
A treasure trove of tips and advice, how-to guides and projects.

www.gardenersworld.com
Gardening advice from the experts on seasonal plants and projects with step-by-step guides and blogs.

www.gardentrading.co.uk
Offers a nostalgic range of garden storage items and furniture – from apple stores to herb pots.

www.gardenvisit.com
Find the best variety of gardens and nurseries to visit locally.

www.nestbox.co.uk
Offers a comprehensive range of nesting boxes for British birds and small mammals, as well as insect and squirrel feeders.

www.rhs.org.uk
The Royal Horticultural Society provides good solid advice on a variety of common gardening queries, news of shows and events, and online shopping.

www.rspb.org.uk
The Royal Society for the Protection of Birds has a great advice section on how to attract all kinds of wildlife into your garden.

www.rspca.org.uk
The Royal Society for the Prevention of Cruelty to Animals website has some helpful pet care tips for ducks, geese, chickens and goats.

www.thebalconygardener.com
Everything you need to create a relaxing, urban oasis – even in the smallest of spaces.

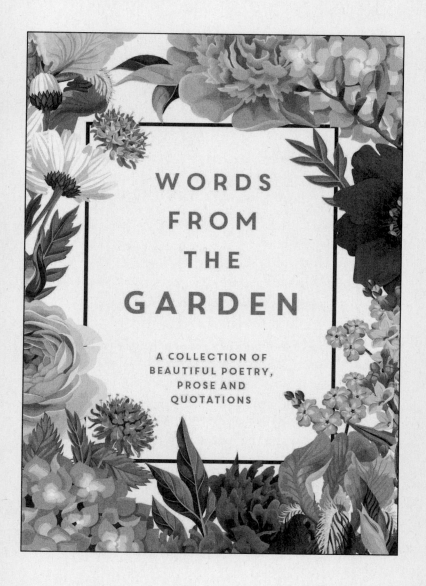

WORDS FROM THE GARDEN

A COLLECTION OF BEAUTIFUL POETRY, PROSE AND QUOTATIONS

WORDS FROM THE GARDEN

A Collection of Beautiful Poetry, Prose and Quotations

Isobel Carlson

ISBN: 978-1-78685-489-6

Hardback

£7.99

'The soul cannot thrive in the absence of a garden.'

Thomas Moore

This beautiful collection of poetry and prose through the seasons rhapsodises on the spectacle of colour and everything green and flourishing in the garden. The perfect book for a moment's reflection, whether you are cooped up on a rainy day in your potting shed or admiring the fruits of your labour on a sunny evening from the pergola.

GARDENING
HACKS

Handy Hints to Make Gardening Easier

Seedling for
your Monday
detox salad

Eggshell
from your
Friday fry-up

Dan Marshall

Over **130** amazing hacks inside!

GARDENING HACKS
Handy Hints to Make Gardening Easier

Dan Marshall

ISBN: 978-1-78685-258-8

Paperback

£9.99

- Do you spend hours on garden maintenance, leaving no time for the fun stuff?

- Would you like the chance to eat your produce before the pests get to them?

- Do you dream of an abundant garden that's beautiful all year round?

These and dozens of other gardening dilemmas are solved with this trusty guide filled with ingenious gardening hacks. Whether you're a regular Best In Show looking for some time-saving tips or you've just planted your first seedlings and you want to learn more, *Gardening Hacks* is your fully illustrated manual to blossoming as a gardener.

The Gardener's Year

Pippa Greenwood

THE GARDENER'S YEAR

Pippa Greenwood

ISBN: 978-1-84953-658-5

Hardback

£9.99

This beautifully illustrated guide contains specific month-by-month 'to do' lists for ornamental gardens, edible crops and general maintenance, as well as tips on things to look out for, such as pests and how to eliminate them. With diary pages for making your own notes each month, this pocket-sized calendar is a must-have whether you're a seasoned gardener or just starting out.

If you're interested in finding out more about our books,
find us on Facebook at Summersdale Publishers
and follow us on Twitter at @Summersdale.

www.summersdale.com